Praise for Agnes Vojta

"*The Eden of Perhaps* is equal parts vulnerable and fierce with a subtle touch of humor, a deep twist of desire, and twin scoops of heartache and hope. A moving collection of poems for women on the edge of breaking open, standing on the ledge of possibility, their hearts in their hands."

—Molly Remer, *Brigid's Grove*

"John Gardner once said that there are only two basic plots: a stranger comes to town and a person goes on a trip. In her strong new collection, Agnes Vojta takes her readers on a trip which moves from the personal to the mythic. Her tone ranges from pensive to giddy, but she is always bringing the reader, *out/into the world/towards adventure.*

—Mike James, author of *Jumping Drawbridges in Technicolor* and *Parades*

"In *The Eden of Perhaps*, Agnes Vojta explores identity through poems of hunger, atonement, and transformation. In her poem "Muse" she discovers *One day the universe / had enough of me / not listening… woke me up with a sonic boom…and shouted What are you waiting for?* In "Rules for Pruning," she observes *So, in cutting back, / you shape the future.* In "Alter Ego," she confesses *life was simpler / before she / appeared.* Ultimately, she finds a quiet triumph in accepting and loving *the woman she wants to become.* Rather than consuming one and moving on to the next, these meditations are meant to be held on the tongue and savored."

—Dianne Borsenik, author of *Raga for What Comes Next* (Stubborn Mule Press, 2019)

More praise for Agnes Vojta:

"I was in a workshop once, and someone described a poem as *miraculous*. I found this very silly. Poems aren't miracles! They can't cure cancer! But upon reading *Eden of Perhaps*, I am beginning to see their point. I don't mean God (Vojta, not God, wrote this book), but that something that should not be possible is. Poems that weave in Mythology, physics, hiking, questions, loss should not work, but here we are anyways."

"Vojta writes *Questioning feels dangerous. / Not knowing unbearable,* which I find to be true of most things, but the reverse is the case here. Questioning why these poems work feels unbearable, not knowing feels dangerous, especially when one has the delightful task of being asked to blurb the book. So I'll just say this: I started this book with every intention of taking my time. I had a plan /to make it last. But I must confess, I read it all in one go. And so should you. Then we can both read it again together."

—Nadia Wolnisty, EIC of *Thimble Literary Magazine*, author of *A Zoo* (Finishing Line Press), *Signs Taken for Wonders* (Dancing Girl Press), *Manual* (Cringe Worthy Poets), and *You Got To Let It Go before It Takes You Over* (Spartan).

The Eden of Perhaps

Poems by Agnes Vojta

Kansas City   Missouri

Spartan Press
Kansas City, MO
spartanpresskc.com

Copyright © Agnes Vojta, 2020
First Edition 1 3 5 7 9 10 8 6 4 2
ISBN: 978-1-952411-00-7
LCCN: 2020934117

Design, edits and layout: Jason Ryberg
Cover and title page images: Agnes Vojta
Author photo: Agnes Vojta
All rights reserved. No part of this publication may be reproduced or transmitted in any form or by any means, electronic or mechanical, including photocopying, recording or by info retrieval system, without prior written permission from the author.

Acknowledgements:

I thank everybody who inspired and supported me as I was writing these poems. My special gratitude goes to the women who permitted me to use their stories and words in "The World Splits Open".

I thank the editors of the publications where some of these poems have first appeared, sometimes in different form or under a different title:

Ariel Chart: "We live in a World of Right Angles," "Apparition," "Riddled,"
As it Ought to Be Magazine: "Sisyphus Calls It Quits,"
Black Coffee Review: "Running away with the Circus,"
Former People: "My Battery is Low," "We, the Argonauts,"
Gasconade Review: "Alea Iacta Est," "Peace of the River,"
Gyroscope Review: "Never too Late,"
Mad Swirl: "Suffering is not a Competition,"
Minute Magazine: "Lesson from a Dandelion,"
Nixes Mate Review: "Unsaid," "Lifeline,"
Red River Review: "How to Walk on Slickrock,"
    "Train to Uncertainty,"
The Blue Nib: "Ritual,"
Thimble Literary Magazine: "Before a Winter,"
    "At the Crossroads,"
Trailer Park Quarterly: "Greeting Cards They Don't Make"

TABLE OF CONTENTS

Muse / 1

We Live in a World of Right Angles / 2

What If / 3

Apparition / 4

Alter Ego / 5

Questioning / 6

Secret / 7

One Does not Miss the Undiscovered Country / 8

Seeds of No Return / 9

Atonement / 10

Unlabeled / 11

Never too Late / 12

Smalltalk is Wading in the Shallows / 13

Theater of Shadows / 14

Accomplished Hamster / 16

Running away with the Circus / 17

The Cage / 18

Invisible / 19

Greeting Cards They Don't Make / 20

The World Splits Open / 21

Train to Uncertainty / 22

My Battery Is Low and It's Getting Dark / 23

Cracked / 24

Bitter Stones / 25

Ritual / 26

Unconditional / 27

Lifeline / 28

At the Crossroads / 29

Riddled / 30

Before a Winter / 31

Triptych on Highway 28 / 32

Suffering is not a Competition / 34

We, the Argonauts / 35

Fountain Pen / 36

Pictures at an Exhibition / 37

Fortunate Magnolia / 41

Under Construction / 42

Rapunzel Has Enough / 43

Sleeping Beauty Wakes Up / 44

In Defense of Compartmentalization / 46

Lesson from a Dandelion / 47

Meditations / 48

Peace of the River / 50

How to Walk on Slickrock / 51

Garden Wisdom / 52

Teach Me / 54

Emancipation / 56

Alea Iacta Est / 57

Song for the Woman I Want to Become / 58

The Eden of Perhaps

Muse

One day, the universe
had enough of me
not listening
to the gentle hints
and sent a special kind of muse –

not one of the wispy muses
who whisper in the trees,
not one of the melancholy muses
who haunt bars at closing time,
not one of the cerebral muses
who linger in libraries,

but a fierce, fiery muse
of the get-their-attention squad
who came thundering in,
woke me up with a sonic boom,
turned my life upside down
and me inside out,
and shouted –

What are you waiting for?

We Live in a World of Right Angles

where the shortest distance
between two points
is a straight line,
and a statement
is either true or false,
and you can reason
your way out of the labyrinth.

But what if the labyrinth
no longer has a solution,
and Ariadne's thread
frayed and tangled
into an impossible knot?

I am sick of graph paper grids.
I want to round
the squares, sink
into softness, dissolve
the man-made, melt
into the in-between.

What If

What if we didn't take dictation
from false dichotomies,
and our destination
is really here?

What if the liminal spaces
are dwelling places,
the grassy strip between
the demarcation lines,
that no-woman's land,
a field of possibility?

What if we could rest
in the beauty of dusk
between day and night,
in the grey between black and white?

What if we could see
the infinitude of fractions
span the chasm between one and zero
like a rainbow for us to walk on?

What if the answer is not
here/there, either/or, but:
both,
between,
and?

Apparition

Three mornings,
the fox appeared
at dawn,
a sign
whose magic meaning
I cannot decipher.

Three nights,
you burrowed
into my dreams,
leaving me disquieted,
confused by answers
to questions
I did not know I had.

Alter Ego

I split open,
and a person burst forth
whom I did not know.

She and I are slowly
getting acquainted.

She is exciting
and frightening
and has much to teach me,

but sometimes I wish
I could shove her
in the back of a closet

and forget
her existence.

Life was simpler
before she
appeared.

Questioning

The stacks of library books
reveal what torments her.
The receipts with their due dates
chronicle a journey.

She cannot find in her town
what she seeks; she orders
through interlibrary loan.
The computer does not judge.

She avoids eye contact
when she picks up the books
and is relieved the librarian
has an unfamiliar face.

At home, she hides them
under piles of paper
or on the shelves,
spines facing the wall.

She reads only
when she is alone in the house.
Questioning feels dangerous.
Not knowing unbearable.

Secret

I pretend the door
at the end of the hallway
is not there. I keep
the key hidden
in a hollow space
of my heart.
I won't tell what I store
in that chamber.

I visit furtively
and rarely,
lest I won't be allowed
to leave again.
Already, coming out,
I am not the same me
who went in.

One Does not Miss the Undiscovered Country

We miss the land from which we're exiled, miss
the shore we left to which we can't return,
miss what we had, and mourn what might have been.

We do not miss the undreamed, whose existence
our wildest fantasies have not imagined,
the summits never glimpsed on the horizon,
the unmapped realms of which no stories tell.

But once we spot, from highest mast, the mountains
that rise up, far, where ocean meets the sky,
we yearn to walk their slopes and can't believe
we ever lived, content, without them.

Seeds of No Return

I feast on fantasies,
ban the word *never*
from my mind and let
imagination wing me

to the Eden of *perhaps*.
I indulge in daydreams,
savor each juicy thought
like a luscious fruit,

but I am afraid
to taste the forbidden
pomegranate, to eat
the seeds of no return.

Atonement

Sometimes I wish I belonged
to a religion that practices confession.

I can walk in the forest and confess to the trees,
kneel by the river and whisper to the water,
stand in the field and shout to the sky –
but who will pronounce me shriven?

I have to prescribe my own penance,
whip my body to exhaustion to drown out
the mind's self-flagellation,

and wait for the unpromised peace.

Unlabeled

I reject your labels.
I do not wish to appropriate
a designation I do not deserve,
a badge I did not earn.

I can tell you what dreams
fuel my days and what longings
my nights. I cannot
tell you what that makes me.

I am both particle and wave,
oscillate between the poles,
span the continuum of frequencies.
I do not fit into your boxes.

I am the compass needle that points
wherever the magnet is.
You cannot use my orientation
to define North.

Never too Late

Do not mock
the traveler who starts out late
on her journey. She carries
the burden of decades
and the weight of missed opportunities.

Her first step
is as significant as yours was,
but it costs her more courage
to challenge her beliefs
about who she is: it calls
her entire life into question,
and she wonders
whether it is already too late.

But do not pity her, either.
Cheer her on in her quest.
Tell her that growing
is brave and beautiful,
and that it is never
too late.

Smalltalk is Wading in the Shallows

Sometimes we just want
to feel cool water
around our ankles,
be refreshed,
but not committed
to more than cold feet.

Sometimes we wade deeper
and learn where boulders lurk,
where deep holes gape,
where quicksand waits,
until we are all in
and give ourselves
to the current.

And sometimes we abandon
caution and jump,
risk bruises and cuts,
the price for being one
with the river
without reservations,
without holding
anything back.

Theater of Shadows

I
We each tow
the iceberg of our past,
cragged below
the surface of time.

What we know
of one another
fills a thimble;
we yearn
to share oceans.

II
How do we tell the stories
of tangled lives? We never
start at the beginning;

we pull loops from the skein
without digging for the end
of the thread.

We weave patches
and stitch them together
without a pattern

to a crazy quilt
that will never
be complete.

III
We are actors
in a theater of shadows
where we only see
one another's projections,
distorted
by the slant of light.

Accomplished Hamster

Her well-oiled wheel whirrs
smoothly and efficiently.
She is a perfect, accomplished hamster,

but the more she runs, the less
she gets anywhere,
and she screams in her dreams.

She thinks about jumping off,
but is scared of landing
on unknown ground.

Her spirit makes barely a sound
as it is crushed
under the wheel.

Running away with the Circus

I want to run away
with the circus
but I have no skills:

I am not agile enough
to swing from a trapeze,
too clumsy to juggle,
afraid of lions –

> but perhaps I am sad
> enough to be a clown.

I can be a sad clown
in a derelict small town circus
where feet have worn dusty paths
between tattered tents.

At least it would be different
from being a respectable
middle aged wife with a house
and two kids who are grown
and a job I am so good at,
I can fake it while my mind
is already off with the caravan.

The Cage

She constructs
the cage carefully,
crafts the bars
with precision,
polishes the lock
to perfection.

Her wings
do not fit inside.
She cuts them off.

Then she proudly
watches the door
swing shut.

Invisible

She slips through
the days unnoticed.

She wants to hoist
a neon flag
to the world:
Here I am! Over here!
jump up and down
wave her arms
like a castaway
signaling a ship

but her flailing
remains unseen
her shouting unheard
and the ship sails
undeterred
past her island.

Greeting Cards They Don't Make

— for Pam Crabtree

I tried to find a card for you.
Get well soon sounds fine
for the flu or the leg you broke walking the dog.
It doesn't cut it
for fist shaped bruises.

I opened "Caring thoughts":
May only peaceful memories
touch your heart today
is a tall order when you're dictating
(can't write with that concussion)
your statement for the prosecutor.

The goodness in you brings out the goodness
in everyone around you
is just insulting.
It obviously didn't in him.
And *Give all your worries and cares to God?*
Yeah, you've tried that one for years.

I am sick of hearts and of angels.
I want a card that shouts
You're a strong woman,
and we love you,
and we hope the bastard rots in jail.

It would be a bestseller.

The World Splits Open
*—What would happen if one woman told the truth about her life?
The world would split open.*

>—Muriel Rukeyser

We sat in the circle and listened
as our sisters tried to put
the unspeakable into words
that, slowly, pushed their way
through the sobs,

and our tears mingled
as we held each other
and heard

how you wanted to kill yourself,
how you mourn your dead babies,
how you were drugged and raped,

and a long silence fell

until one spoke

> *This is the sound
> of women sending love
> and compassion.
> We should record it.*

Train to Uncertainty

While you still question
your destination
and can't decide
to buy your ticket,

the conductor slams
the door shut,
blows the whistle,
and the engine
pulls out of the station.

You are left
on an empty platform
with a suitcase
full of regrets.

You should have jumped
on the speeding train
to uncertainty

that would at least
have been going
somewhere.

My Battery Is Low and It's Getting Dark
— last words of the Mars rover Opportunity

When we cannot admit
to our real pain
and dust chokes our words,

we weep over the Mars rover,
the robot who epitomizes
loneliness,

who left tracks
in the dystopian landscape
of a surrealist painting,

with not even
a faceless shrouded figure
as companion.

Cracked

The thin veneer of clarity
cracked and revealed tumult.

I want to shed my self
like a snake sheds her skin.

Words lie coiled inside me,
ready to spring.

Bitter Stones

The unsaid words
are bitter stones
in my mouth.

Do you know
the world's saddest word?
Never.

Ritual

Give me your pain
and I will fashion it a shrine.
I will craft a reliquary
for your tears.
I will build a temple
to your suffering

where gods of stone
turn their silent faces
to the wall

and the altar
holds nothing but a knife
and a burnished bowl.

I will bare my wrist
and be both celebrant
and sacrifice.

Unconditional

I want to purify
my love for you,
cleanse it
of all expectations,
of all desires,
of all that is about me,

until it runs clear
like spring water
that I pour for you
when you are thirsty,
without asking
anything in return,

and you can
accept it from me
without second thoughts,
as you do not question
the spring that flows
in unconditional abundance.

Lifeline

Instead of calling
the suicide hotline,
you make an appointment
to get a haircut:

you know that your sense
of responsibility
won't allow you
to stand up your stylist.

At the Crossroads

Rest on the rocks,
feel their reassuring solidity,

take a deep breath to still
the panic that rises like bile,

recite the litany
against fear

and imagine
Sisyphus happy.

Riddled

I knelt by the river
and looked
for a smooth stone
with a hole,

but the rock I found
was rough and riddled
with a network
of passages

sifting light and water,
sandstone worn
to fragile bridges
that are barely holding.

Before a Winter

Precariously,
the sycamores perch
on the river bank.

Tangled roots,
unearthed,
claw the gravel.

Yellow leaves litter
the ground
like unanswered letters.

Triptych on Highway 28

I
The snow laden sky hangs heavy,
as if bowing under a burden
of unconfessed sins
it cannot discharge.

Pregnant clouds
drag their swollen bellies
over fallow fields
that lie waiting for absolution.

II
I am driving
toward the rainbow.
The road runs straight
for seven miles,
and ahead, in the black February sky,
is the most vibrant rainbow
I have ever seen.

I am alone in the car,
singing and crying
at the same time
and bubbling

with anticipation
as I am heading
to the rainbow's end.

III
It is raining again,
and the water
pools on the road.
Black-eyed Susan
and Queen Anne's lace
stand upright
in the soggy fields.

I pull off the highway
onto a gravel road,
stop the car
and get out
to pick flowers
in the rain,
don't care
that I get soaked:

I need to convince myself
that I have not yet
given up.

Suffering is not a Competition

There are no judges who weigh
grief against grief,
no trophies for the heaviest burden,
no ribbons for the most deserving despair.
Do not compare.

You must pull
yourself out of the swamp
by your own hair,
declare yourself healed.

There will be no spectators
applauding at the finish line,
no paparazzi snapping,
no journalists waiting
for an interview –

only you
will know
that you've made it,
with nothing to show
than your heart still beating.

We, the Argonauts

We crawled from our boats,
tired from drifting through chaos,
to rest on an island in space and time:
tonight, we are safe.

We are a haphazard band of travelers,
each carrying our own scars,
our personal brand of crazy,
our deep humanity,
and our flawed loves.

For a while, we are companions
in a fellowship of seekers,
look for answers at the bottom
of the river or the bottle
or in the inscrutable face
of the oblivious moon.

Perhaps the golden fleece
is just a phantom,
and we are meant to remain here,
where the river flows in steady blessing
and night is a symphony of frog song.

Fountain Pen

Idle for years, you dried up
like an unused mind,
your nib scabbed,
former fluidity forgotten.

It takes many attempts
to break up the crust.
You scrape the paper,
leaving hesitation marks,

until all clots dissolve and,
with ever bolder strokes,
you bleed yourself free
in a river of words.

Pictures at an Exhibition
  — *after paintings by Greg Edmondson*

I: A Necklace Made of Knives

Your defenses are more effective
than a necklace made of knives:
a shield forged from trauma,
a mail shirt fashioned from past pain,
an invisibility cloak woven from addiction –
impenetrable, they defeat
the knight who approaches
your fortress,
who would have battled the blades
with her bare hands.

II: Those Sweet Sticky Summer Nights

when everything is in bloom
are drenched in honeysuckle.
The moon hangs like a blood orange
above the river. The cicadas
compete with the guitar, the air
clings to our skin, and the night
is pregnant with desires
and misunderstandings.

III: That Summer We Spent Rolling in the Grass

Shaking with laughter,
we rolled down the pasture,
all the way to the river
that magical summer.
On moonlight floats, we traded
poems and stories,
laid on the gravel bar
and wished on stars,
and I was drunk
with dreams and with you.

But perhaps
that summer never was,
all these moments
live just in my imagination,
and we never
got to roll in the grass,
you sail a distant river,
and hay bales rest
in the autumn fields,
where the unsaid words
shrivel and wither.

IV: The Hundred Year Flood

Water, water everywhere;
nothing here is stable,
but the moon sickle sinks
her tendrils into our hearts.
Roots reach
below the diluvian chaos,
anchor us
to the terra firma
that is down there,
somewhere –
we sense it
in our memories,
in our dreams.

V: Sisyphus Calls It Quits

To walk away
from what was your purpose
for all this time;
to simply let the boulder lie
and say: I am
punished enough;
to turn your back,
and not stay any longer
with the impossible
is the impossible.
We have imagined
you happy
with the struggle
towards the height,
or rather tried
to imagine how
it could have filled your heart.

Now depart
from the mountain
without backward glance
and dance
on the bones of the gods
who never deserved
your obedience in the first place.

Fortunate Magnolia

Why did they plant the magnolia
in the corner between the house
and the garage? There is no room for a tree.

Each spring, she blooms valiantly;
each summer, she stretches her branches
with the large leathery leaves over the roof;

you cut them. Last year,
I cried. The blossoms
unfold in front of my window.

Today, the more fortunate magnolias
already in full bloom,
she holds out a few pink buds like fingers,

and the mutilated trunk sprouts shoots,
and there is almost hope
that something new may, once again, grow.

Under Construction

I am not broken.
I do not need to be fixed.
I am just temporarily
under construction.

I am my own survey crew,
study my landscape,
redraw boundary lines,
prepare the ground.

There will be detours,
bumps, and blasting
while I deconstruct
and rebuild myself.

You may not recognize me
when I am done
and my spires
reach the sky.

Rapunzel Has Enough

Strands of hair drop
onto the floor
as chunks of her old life
fall away, and a new
shape emerges,
cropped to its essence.

Her load lightened,
she feels braver,
and her shoulders sprout
the foreshadowings of wings.

Sleeping Beauty Wakes Up

She sits up, rubs her eyes
and wonders: why is it so quiet?
She climbs down the spiral staircase.
Her feet on the stone tiles
make the only sound.

The cooks are asleep in the kitchen.
King and queen are asleep on their thrones.
The knights are asleep standing guard.
She pokes one of them; he does not stir.
She giggles.

Out the window, she sees
the hedge of thorns.

She looks down her gown,
velvet and lace,
pauses for a moment
tiptoes to the squires' room.
She opens the wooden chest,
finds breeches, a tunic, a cloak.
And boots.
She kicks off her satin slippers,
unlaces her dress,
lets it crumple on the floor.

She puts on the squire's clothes.
Her heart beats faster.

Her hands shake a little
as she pushes open
the heavy door and starts
walking across the drawbridge.
She feels strangely giddy,
as if intoxicated
by an exhilarating secret.

As she reaches the hedge,
the thorns part to let her pass,
and she walks out,
into the world,
towards adventure.

In Defense of Compartmentalization

I tried to dissolve
the boundaries, blend
the facets of my life
like a watercolor,
but the paints would not
flow together
and left shapeless blobs.

Perhaps I am meant
to be a mosaic,
my personae
clean edged tiles
of different colors
that live in harmony
next to each other
and do not attempt
to absorb their neighbor
or blur the lines.

That, too, could make
a beautiful picture.

Lesson from a Dandelion

How easily
the dandelions let go –
the brush of a breeze
sets the seeds free.

They float away,
leaving small scars
on the green body
where they once anchored.

I want to learn
not to cling
to those who must leave
when the time comes,

watch them drift
towards growth,
the scars a reminder
how much I loved.

Meditations

I
Goals for today:

Accomplish nothing.
Slow down to arrive.
Practice stillness.
Empty the mind
so the soul can fill.

Pay attention.
Write to remember.
Write to forget.
Learn from the river.
Fall to pieces
so you can be rebuilt.

II
The highway is hemmed
in white and yellow:
daisies and sunflowers.

I want to stop,
take a picture
to keep them forever,

but the windy road
has no shoulder,
no place to pull over.

In searching, I fail to see;
in trying to hold on,
I lose.

III
Mist rises from the lake,
hides the clear water,
as fog clouds my mind.

I long to follow the raven
who silently parts
the veil with his wings,

fly toward a destiny
I cannot yet see,
or maybe just fly

for the sake of flying,
and not wish,
and not want.

Peace of the River

I want to spend a year by the river
and live in her seasons, wake and sleep
each day to her music, smell her mood.

I would be up early to see the mists
rise from the water and to watch
the great heron wade in the shallows.

I would walk on the banks at dusk
when the shadows lengthen and wait
for the bats to emerge from the cliffs.

I would listen to the muddy torrent
that rages after the winter rains
and warns me to keep my distance

and to her languid green summer voice
that beckons me to throw myself into her arms,
trusting her to carry me past the jungled bluffs.

I would let myself be cleansed and blessed,
the peace of the river would fill my soul,
and I would have to stay forever.

How to Walk on Slickrock

Trust your brain
and feet to read,
instinctively,
the interplay of gravity
and friction.

Do not second-guess
whether you will be able
to walk down
the steep slope.

Commit to your step
without hesitation.
Put your full weight
on your feet,
walk erect,
with determination.
It's the only way.

When you start
crouching in fear,
that's when you slide.

Garden Wisdom

– for Mimi Hedl

I: On Centering

Fill the wheelbarrow
so that the weight
rests right above the axle.
Feel how much easier
it is to push the load.

II: Doing without Doing

Let the hammer fall
under its own weight.
Let gravity drive
the stake into the ground.

III: Rules for Pruning

Be bold!

Remove the dead,
the damaged,
the diseased.

Use a sharp tool,
make a clean cut.

Where branches overlap
and rub their bark,
choose one,

but leave a little
of the one you cut
to ward off rot.

You have the power to decide
which way new growth will go:
the last branch that you leave
will give direction.

So, in cutting back,
you shape the future.

Teach Me

Teach me to do outrageous things,
to jump in the abyss
and grow my wings
as I fall. Teach me
to go all in,
to commit without fear.
Teach me to hear
what the universe whispers.

Teach me to let go with grace
to face the uncertainty,
not to cling to security.
Teach me to sing
when the pain is too deep.
When I want the long sleep
slap me, wake me, shake me
out of despondency
out of complacency
out of this saturated, overfed life.

Teach me what it means to be free,
to be me, to throw
the world's expectations on a pyre,
to become the fire
that liberates, animates,
recreates me.

Teach me that only I hold me back,
that I hold the deck
and deal my own hands.
Teach me to dance
on the precipice.

Teach me to fly, to cry,
to dream, to scream—
whether nobody listens
or the whole world,
teach me
to not give a damn.

Emancipation

She has come of age. She escaped
the guardianship of her stern older sister
who plans her life with a straightedge.

She is the meanderer who discovers
delicious detours and does not flinch
when the briars cut her skin.

She is the story seeker and word weaver,
dream dancer and rooftop shouter,
who does not care to appear ordinary.

She is the cliff diver and dragon tamer,
fire walker and forbidden-fruit-eater
and sometimes gets in trouble and has to be

rescued by her sensible sister
who watches over her, worried and amazed,
and with a twinge of jealousy.

Alea Iacta Est

I lingered
on the banks of the Rubicon
as if it were the River Styx
and I afraid of the final ferry ride,

but the die was cast
the moment I admitted to myself
what I had carried deep inside,
and started speaking it,
softly and with hesitation,

and I crossed the Rubicon,
and instead of dim Asphodel Meadows,
green fields with unforged paths
lay waiting.

Song for the Woman I Want to Become

She paints her life in bold brush strokes:
pomegranate love, obsidian pain.
She is not afraid to start over.

She won't let herself be silenced.
She owns her stage and shouts her truth.
Her songs come from the heart and the gut.

She has dived in deep wells,
clawed her way back to the surface
and emerged filled with compassion.

She carries her scars with dignity
and faces her demons with courage.
She is resilient as water.

She can no longer be tamed;
she bursts her banks like the river,
flowing and flooding, fierce and fearless.

She is honest as the ocean,
loyal as the sunrise,
and I love her.

Agnes Vojta grew up in Germany, spent a few years in California, Oregon, and England, and now lives in Rolla, Missouri where she teaches physics at Missouri S&T. Her first poetry collection *Porous Land* was published in 2019 by Spartan Press.

This project was made possible, in part, by generous support from the Osage Arts Community.

Osage Arts Community provides temporary time, space and support for the creation of new artistic works in a retreat format, serving creative people of all kinds — visual artists, composers, poets, fiction and nonfiction writers. Located on a 152-acre farm in an isolated rural mountainside setting in Central Missouri and bordered by ¾ of a mile of the Gasconade River, OAC provides residencies to those working alone, as well as welcoming collaborative teams, offering living space and workspace in a country environment to emerging and mid-career artists. For more information, visit us at www.osageac.org

www.ingramcontent.com/pod-product-compliance
Lightning Source LLC
Chambersburg PA
CBHW030351100526
44592CB00010B/912